The Very Word

Barry Clegg

ISBN: 978-1-989403-16-7 (paperback)

Published by:
Barry Clegg
barrygclegg@gmail.com

Cover image & design:
Leslie Cooper

Layout by:
thepublishingmentor.com

For my wife, Leslie

Acknowledgments

It was the music of Benjamin Britten that first got me interested in poetry. Its superb song cycles and choral works draw upon English poetry from the 13th century to the 20th.

In many cake-and-tea-fueled discussions of poetry and literature, Wayne Tompkins shared freely his prodigious knowledge and enthusiasm. He raised the bar with many a ruthless comment on my work.

Susan Wolff also offered insights and encouragement that made me hurry back to the computer.

My wife Leslie, sister Suma, daughters Alison and Joni, and stepsons Robert and Graeme make up the emotional context in which I have been moved to write, and have been generous enough to take a critical interest in my work.

Preface

As I am an engineer by education, my passions for classical music and literature have surprised some people. I'm not sure why: I have many engineer friends with similar interests.

A keen reader from childhood, I came to writing first through technical writing; then to humorous writing for the sheer fun of it; and finally, usually in response to feelings aroused by love, nature, nature loss, or some humorous surge.

Poetry to me is a condensed form of communication intended for reading, listening to, and looking at. Good poetry is worth revisiting time after time, and it has the advantage – over symphonies and novels – that this takes only minutes.

Several of the poems in this book are based on personal experience, though I often allow a sort of poetic truth to override mere facts.

Many of the poems as presented here were touched up in haste before the merciless calendar of the Coronavirus.

Contents

Another World

He'd probably never heard of Fathers' Day,
that quiet English June afternoon in 1970:
it was the afternoon an astronaut

plodded up the garden path,
in helmet, gauntlets, boots, and
suit the blue-black of deep space.

Bellona leapt instinctively
and struck the invader
amidships with her dagger-fangs.

Shouts from my father
more fierce than the dog itself,
whose barking aroused

a clamour of demented puppies.
Father was indignant. Are you all right?
Here… Removal of helmet, loosening of belt.

Good, no blood. Can I get you a gin and tonic?
Not allowed, sir,
while in charge of the motorcycle.

What motorcycle?
What are you doing here anyway?
Telegram, sir.

(*contd.*)

For me?
Are you William Clegg?
I am – let's have a look.

HAPPY FATHERS' DAY,
he read out. Ah, my
new-Canadian children at work.

The pups fell upon each other –
growling and snarling in readiness
for further invasions.

A Survivor's Birthday

That year's best wishes
were mocked by cruel
ups and downs.

It was impossible
not to change after the
unfairground rides we braved.

I treasure
what we have become
as I had treasured what we were,

and prize as never before
the future's million present moments.

A Welcome Storm

That night it seemed we were
paying for the recent sunny days.
Thunder tumbled from the peaks
into our Alpine village and boomed
across the lake. Rain pelted rooftops,
drummed on balconies,
the mountain gods roared.

A car hissed through sudden puddles
while we lay warm and dry
by opened windows. I counted out
the lengthening gaps between flash
and crash, every six seconds
a mile's distance, till all that was left
of the storm was the dripping.

** Mein Deutsch ist alt und klein
und schwach, aber ich muss erklären:
wie wohl ist unser Urlaub, wann
die Blitze blitzen, der Donner donnert,
und ich mit meiner Liebe liege.*

* My German is old and small
and weak, but I must declare:
how pleasant is our holiday, when
the lightning lightens, the thunder thunders,
and I lie down with my love.

Bananas #1

My mother seemed to know everything
about food. In England even after the War
there was little variety and short supply.
She was into health food before anyone

had heard of health food – fed us cereals,
vitamins, malt, home-made yoghourt,
not to mention sundry vegetables
and fruits from the garden.

At different times, to reinforce
the ration book, she kept chickens, ducks,
Old English Game birds, and – nourished
by lawnmower clippings – rabbits.

She read *Look Younger, Live Longer,*
by Gayelord Hauser,
and fifty years later
you could see it had worked.

When I was three
the War ended.
I was given a banana
to celebrate.

Mum said it was important
to chew it slowly and thoroughly.
Perhaps there was some ceremonial
or bodily reason for this.

(contd.)

When she was old, I asked my mother
why we had to eat bananas with such diligence.
She could offer no particular rationale
for mumbling them to death, except maybe

to prolong the banana experience.
In any case, to be on the safe side
I still devote at least five minutes
to any banana that comes my way.

Bananas #2

It was minus twenty.
A young man walking along
the quiet neighbourhood street
held in one raised, gloved hand
the likeness of a banana –
tall as himself.

I had to ask.
What's *that?*

It's a giant stuffed banana.

A cautious pause: then…
What do you do with it?

Nothing, it's just an animal, right?

Ah, I said, treading cautiously
the slippery skin of ignorance.
Five minutes might not be enough
for this banana.

Aha!

Calculus

The summation of infinitesimal differences.

In broken bones set,
crops harvested, busloads
of schoolkids delivered,
in concerts that delight thousands
of fans, there lies conspicuous merit.
No questions asked.

To hold things together against the
centrifugal forces of existence
was his aim at the factory. Crucial as bonds
constraining atoms were the nuts, bolts, and screws
his engineering arts optimized –
and did anyone say, *My car hasn't fallen apart ?*

At the public utility his task was
warming homes through winter,
making computers design networks
to supply gas on even the bittermost days.
Thus he made heating cheaper –
and did anyone say, *The house is so cozy ?*

His job at the government was to raise
understanding by reshaping information,
calling on his every skill
to contrive words that engaged,
illuminated, convinced –
and did anyone say, *Our taxes are well spent ?*

However, however, and however,
his work did provide a boost –
through minuscule contributions –
to fasteners, homes, and taxpayers
in millions upon millions
upon millions.

Cuttyhunk

Through a network of cobbled streets,
luck and intuition deliver us one minute
before departure time – in good time,
it turns out, for a half-hour hiatus while
the mechanic performs some urgent operation.

Wide Awake II, Elizabeth Boat Lines,
Port of New Bedford, Massachusetts,
lies tired and unlovely on the
malodorous wharf water, rocking
like an old dog in its dreams.

We wait. A fellow passenger
with glittering eye stops us to tell
how, back in Moby Dick days,
tunnels from nearby taverns funneled
shanghaied sailors onto whaling ships.

But here (if the T-shirt's really his)
comes Captain Smart,
with authentic gusty grey beard
and turbulent belly. He invites us aboard,
boasting we're now ahead of schedule.

In the cabin below, severe rows of benches,
the diesel engine's penetrating clatter.
Squinting against the smell of oil, I inspect
Fire Station No. 3 – a groping clasp sans hose,
sans axe, sans extinguisher, sans everything.

(contd.)

On deck, a braver world. Who can ignore
the sea sky? This day unstinting azure,
with cotton wool accents, and three
incongruous parallel vapour trails,
fading stigmata of a phantom fly-past.

The sea's a roiling threat of ebony and blue,
except for our flamboyant churning tail.
Yet how flat the further waters look,
how untrustworthy their
intimation of calm.

The coiled rope I'm sitting on
has damped my holiday pants,
salt spray is crisping my skin.
It does me good to stand and
take the ocean's heave into my legs.

I watch a distant ship sink
below the horizon, not slowly
shrink from the eye's reach
as flat-earth landlubbers
might expect.

Discreet clouds appear, to chaperone
a necklace of mellifluous islands
decorating the skyline. The chart names
Naushon, Uncatena, Nashawena, Penikese,
Nonamesset, Cuttyhunk, and Pasque.

My binoculars slice the distance
into planes of stage scenery.
A treeless island shakes in their
magic circle, rocks are grazing sheep,
buildings wait like crofters' shacks.

At length the ferry closes with Cuttyhunk,
ties up to screams of hawsers, capstans,
gulls. We gather our things for
a quick ride across the bay – but after
so long a passenger I find myself

compelled to exertion, and leave
the shore party to their small boat. I swim
a plodding stroke from mooring to mooring,
splash through a patch of lapping seaweed,
and lurch triumphantly ashore.

We get together at the souvenir shop.
Our substantial haul includes
for me one Cuttyhunk sweatshirt,
vibrant with the mondrian exuberance
of signal flags. A perfect fit.

Dead Shot

I have seen in movies a man
galloping across rocky terrain
fire over his shoulder and strike
his pursuer's gun to the ground.

I have seen a man pin
his enemy's hand to the bar
with a knife thrown quicker
than a pistol drawn.

And I have seen a man
shoot the claws
off an eagle
in flight.

Today's police too often lack
the skill to wound – despite a certain knack
for stopping unarmed suspects
with six bullets in the back.

Disgrace

Benedictus benedicat

Latin graces bookended our paltry meals.
Forbidden to eat before the first or after the second,
we did not understand why complicated rulings
in a dead language stood above our hunger.

Indeed there was much to be explained.
The flag of Reason fluttered uneasily
in the pontifical winds agitated by
our headmaster. Little of grace
brightened Bruto's boarding school.

He inflicted punishment with a bogus reluctance
that could not conceal his gratification.
In full view of us all Bruto would grab
some supposed miscreant by the cheeks,
intoning, "Bow your head in woe, boy,
bow your head in woe!"

His nose for weakness inspired many a mocking
nickname that stuck pitilessly for years.
Big Teeth, Scoffer, Tubby, Sunday School –
did these unfortunate boys grow up bullies,
or learn to scorn Bruto's example?

We imagined revelations
in a school magazine…

Shameful Secrets of Teaching Staff…

Some new boys were reduced to tears
or bed-wetting – but most learned to accept
the nasty microcosm chosen for them
by well-meaning parents.

(contd.)

Not Puggy, though –
                    Puggy jumped:
at night from a second-floor window, fled
miles through the countryside before
being captured. His courage and desperation
silenced us.

Headmaster Tossed from Building…

Bruto taught a shallow, Anglo-centric
caricature of History. With peace only
ten years old, world maps still boasted
plenty of Empire. Bruto's factoids
were like the red bits of a jigsaw puzzle
missing half its pieces. We enumerated
the kings of England like parrots –
with perhaps equal comprehension.

"1860, *Great Expectations* published," said Bruto.
"1901, death of Queen Victoria."
Before Sunday's walk to the village church,
Bruto pursued our hit-and-miss education.
He'd check the date, then press a solemn penny
for the collection into each boy's hand.
"1940, Battle of Britain."
"1919, Treaty of Versailles."

…1954, Education Woefully Ineffective

Now and then a head expecting to bow
in woe was instead forced to memorize
passages from the Bible.
For some forgotten offense I was set
verses from *The Book of Proverbs*. How unjustly
Chapter 10 begins. *The proverbs of Solomon:*

A wise son maketh a glad father:
but a foolish son is the heaviness of his mother.

Penalties incurred by faulty recall
further shook the nervous system.
Fear and confusion lingered for years,
but to avoid added heaviness
I breathed nothing of this to my parents.

Post-war expectations of discipline and hardship –
as bad or worse at other English boarding schools –
did not lessen the disgrace
of mindless cruelty.

Spoiling the Child…

No rod was spared, but many a child spoilt.
On two occasions Bruto bent me over and delivered
six swingeing strokes of a bamboo cane.

By evening the rippling welts
could almost be borne with honour:
the lasting damage was in my head.
Neither liar nor cheat, thief nor vandal,
no more troublesome or rambunctious
than any twelve-year-old,
I came to believe myself unusually wicked.

Alumnus Dumbstruck…

Some years after advancing to a senior school,
where the depth of my sins was never suspected,
Bruto and I bumped into each other in the street.
"I hear you're going to Cambridge," he smirked.
"How did you wangle that?"
I could not find it in me to speak to this man.

Benedicto benedicatur

Everything Happens for a Reason

I must have been twelve, riding Tilly's bike
up the hill. It was fitted with a derailleur –
a gadget I admired and coveted.
In a low gear for speed on the slope I pedalled hard
and was looking down to watch the chain
slide across the cogwheels when I smashed
into the back of a parked car
and fell to the road.

Tilly caught up quickly.
Look what you've done to my bike!
Here, I said, let me straighten it.
But one wheel curved like an optical illusion
and the frame obstructed the pedals.
Sorry, I didn't see the car there…
You didn't see the car? It's a 2.5 litre Pathfinder!
…because I was watching the gears.

Lifting the front wheel with the disdain
of a boy asked to hold his mother's handbag,
Tilly started the long trudge down town.
I rode my bike home in the opposite direction –
ego seriously injured – and collapsed
onto my bed, mulling miserably
over the stupidest act of my life thus far.

At school the story was repeated with unfriendly glee.
Our teacher shook her wise head and said
to the class, Everything happens for a reason.

For what possible reason did *my* accident happen?
I couldn't see how it benefited anyone.

Perhaps Miss Lawson thought Fate was playing a role –
but why should Fate take any interest in me?

My father came up with five pound-notes.
I had expected a hard time – but remembering
how he had crashed his brother-in-law's
motorbike thirty years earlier, Dad relaxed
into a glow of forgiveness.

I delivered the money to Mrs Tilmouth
with some reluctance. Five pounds was
several years' pocket money in those days.

Tilly had the frame and wheel replaced, and with
a paint job thrown in, his bike was like new.
He did not offer me a test drive.

Looking back, I doubt Miss Lawson meant
I destroyed the bike *because I was facing
the wrong way*. More likely she saw me
as an Instrument of Fate, acting unwittingly
to teach Tilly respect for his possessions;
or him the Instrument of Fate teaching me
respect for stationary vehicles.

Nowadays, I have no doubt that many things
happen for no reason whatever –
yet that was probably the last time
Tilly lent anyone his bike, and certainly
the last time I cycled into a parked car.

Faintly Interesting

They were coming towards me on the sidewalk,
old friends shoulder to shoulder.
Something about their gait suggested
they'd rather flop in the shade
than engage just now with a tedious world.

They trudged closer. I smiled
and tried to catch their eye.
But their thoughts if anywhere
were elsewhere – haughty sniffs
their sole response.

I stepped onto the street
to let them by, two well-fed
black labs out for a constitutional.
The young woman holding
the leashes was on the phone. She
I don't think even saw me pass.

Family Papers

We were walking slowly through the garden,
pausing where he had replanted something,
repaired the fish pond, or reseeded a patch of lawn.

My father was seventy-one – remembering
how we used to pick fruit together,
how I was said to have a good eye
for trimming the boxwood hedge.

He came to a halt, and put a hand on my arm.
        I've prepared all the papers for your mother.
We were by the tree whose small hard pears
had been ammunition in childhood skirmishes.
        Everything she'll need when I die.
What are you talking about, Dad,
you're not going to die!
He was wearing his tweed sports jacket.
        The will, the pension,
            everything I can do that will help her.
You're not going to die.
        Help you children too.

That was our last time together.
Now I am long past seventy-one,
and still working on my papers.

Gifts of Iron

I dreamed a clever man who cared for little but his self
his friends and sometimes those who served him seldom a
finger lifted for the community except his pleasure was at risk.

And watched him ironing endlessly his shirt the sleeves
the collar again the sleeves so that not one wrinkle
should mar his perfect creation.

Now I sit choosing rearranging words smoothing
rhetorical wrinkles striving interminably for
a flawless surface on matters of no great moment.

And agonize over some…
nicety of punctuation search for a telling image
while the larger world unimprovéd shrugs.

Go Away

Stop it! I said but you would not
and I laughed again and folded over
with pain and croaked again
Stop! and was fine for a few seconds –
but caught your eye
and started again to laugh
and felt the forgotten scalpel
beneath the stitches.

Shut up! I shouted
through crippling pangs
Go away! When it hurts
this much the joke is over.
Thank God I'd been sedated
for the operation.

Understand,
I only want to stop hurting
not laughing.
Don't go away I'm better now.
Don't ever go away.

Giving it Hell

Two compact services daily
in the school chapel –
breakfast and dinner for the soul
plus a one-hour feast on Sunday –
made good use of God's time.
The organ, the choir,
the King James Bible, challenged
without overcoming
my religious inertia.

When prefects read the lesson,
we on the wooden pews
sharpened our ears for a bumbled
Jehoshaphat, or the intense quiet of
stage fright, or the robotic dullness
of incomprehension.

My turn came: empowered
by the captive audience,
I declaimed in seventeenth century prose
the Bible stories as if
they had never before been told.

Someone said afterwards: "I like it
when Clegg reads the lesson –
he just stands there and gives it hell!"

Each school term
the Shakespeare Society
read through a play,
with parts taken by a few
prefects and teachers.
At the "performance"

(no audience but ourselves),
strutting, book in hand,
across the entrance hall,
we made what we could
of the flattering acoustics
and our convoluted lines.

Once, I was an old man being visited
in prison. A solid block of text
gave me something to sink my teeth into.
I plunged in, projecting, gesticulating, looking
from one side to another like Olivier himself –
giving it hell in the finest tradition.

From the corner of my eye I saw a small word
in italics at the end of the monologue – probably *Exit*.
I ranted on with gusto. Shakespeare can be fun!
Almost finished, I looked again at that small word –
and saw not *Exit*, but *Dies*.
With thespian powers pumped up to the limit,
I staged a rapid decline and managed to
expire two dozen syllables later.

The play drew to a welcome conclusion,
which we celebrated with curling sandwiches and
warm tea, in a satisfying glow of achievement.

It seemed prudent to say nothing
of my near-life experience.

The Elements

Cows would plod into the river to drink
and cool their feet. I found the storm
had raised the water above my wellingtons –
and on the far side saw something new:
a hollow of tree roots where the bank
had washed away.

It was just possible to squeeze forward
on my stomach. Inside the willow,
under the ground, inches over the flood!
Lazy ripples nudged new-fallen
leaves and twigs downstream.
I kept quite still… hoping for a frog…
No one in the world… could find me.

More than I wanted to tell I wanted
not to tell my secret. That evening
I sneaked back, with matches and a candle.
The friendly flicker hardly helped,
but I thought I saw a centipede.
I must have lain there twenty minutes,
stiffening and chilled –

but in those days before Science
the elements were simple,
and I had them all.

Going to Earth

Boots slapped my legs, fleeing to the river.
The cows lumbered in with udders swinging,
stirring up a ton of clart. Water spilled into
my wellies as I splashed across to the secret place.

Hardly time to wriggle into the cage
of tree roots where soil had been washed away.
I curled up dead still in my lair.

Where the hell did he go?

My hideout under the ground,
inches over the river –
surely no one in the world could…
Fear dried my mouth.

The water soon cleared,
I held my breath tight. If they
didn't find me in five minutes,
they'd go after someone else.

Let there not be a leech.
Hey, sticklebacks! Three, four…
but I couldn't concentrate.

There he is!

Miniatures

Distraction
Hasty walkers blind,
chattering daffodils deaf –
so full of themselves.

Grim Errand
Slicing through night clouds,
a keen yellow scimitar
on some grim errand.

Indignation
How different the world
if indignation were a
clean-burning fuel…

Intent
An old wind-snapped branch
dropped onto a flower bed.
There was no intent.

Winter
Ageing, sickness, or
accidents that outwit them –
winter comes at last.

Youth
The youth orchestra's
guts and gusto – hear how they
scorn mortality.

Haute Cuisine

Prix fixe, messieurs dames?
Le dîner is *simple.*
Soupe, main course, and *dessert,*
toujours – always – *excellent.*

Our "soup of the day" a bowl
of warm *crème de* mushroom
embellished with four small
boules de camembert.

Main course, crackling spit-roast duck
accentué avec Tewkesbury sauce,
accompanied *naturellement* by
a *selection* of fresh *légumes.*

And *enfin,* to end, *gâteaux variés* –
varied cakes *qui charment*
the palate *judicieux.* Gaston
will display his proud trolley.

The wine waiter?
Mais oui – of course!
Un moment,
messieurs dames.

Have You Never Seen a Snowflake?

Reflective on her seventieth birthday, my sister
disturbed an old memory – of Miss Turnbull,
headmistress at a girls' school in England...

Dianne was gazing through dirty windows
at a rare blizzard, rather than at the elderly embodiment
of knowledge and authority at the front of the class.

"Di-ahn," said Miss Turnbull – who of course
knew better than its owner how to say this name –
"have you never seen a snowflake?"

Ignoring the arid invocation of the Scriptures,
so far removed from useful understanding, my sister
had looked away from the dispiriting ranks of desks

into the wide white whirling world,
where the snowstorm tossed unpredictable
flakes with exhilarating freedom,

flakes outwardly uniform, though each
unique – as one student at Carlisle High School,
as one human being among billions.

"Have *you*," she wondered, "ever really *seen* a snowflake?"
Here was perhaps the start of Dianne's life of rebellion
and liberation. For she went on to become an architect,

a horseback rider, rock climber, artist, mother, hat maker,
traveller, writer, gardener, adventurer, singer, counsellor,
caregiver, and cultivator of enduring friendships.

Miss Turnbull, unwitting catalyst
behind this odyssey of enrichment,
would have been astounded.

High Performance

A dozen eight- or nine-year-olds stand
taut in unkind leotards and tights,
the plump turned pudgy, the slim thin.
Feet spread or shyly pigeoned,
backs straight or stooped,
they come in all shapes and sizes.

While Miss Stella demonstrates
in tricky mirror-image,
bashful smiles and a ripple of giggles
play like sun and breeze over
a cluster of wild flowers.
Ready, and... and the girls launch into
their *galop* across the stage.

Concentrating to the tips of their tongues,
toppling from toe-borne heights, they reach
for balance with wavering limbs.
Miss Stella encourages in rhythm,
tireless as she bends to straighten a leg,
tap a shoulder, or raise an arm. The genius
of her smile grants a deeper confidence.

Les Grands Ballets give no greater pleasure
than this village band of dance.
I blink moist eyes...

Then – it's no use, I must try for myself.
I toss my jacket to Miss Stella:
wallet flops to the floor, keys clatter, and
I leap like Baryshnikov onto the stage.

With a triple pirouette and backward spring
I land light as a leaf at Joni's side –
lift her by the waist, balance her
on a raised hand, and start to spin.
Applause breaks out, the pianist grins,
forces a dizzying pace. Joni
holding her head high
weighs nothing. She calls
through the whirling accelerando, *Daddy!*

Someone touches my arm. *Daddy,*
Daddy, was I good?
I rub my eyes and sit up straight. The piano
is silent. Ballerinas and parents are hugging.
Miss Stella's radiance fills the room.
Yes, Joni, you were wonderful!

I Talk to My Clothes

Past seventy-five, frustrated by Parkinson's –
and now the universe of inanimate objects
has turned unkind.

I talk to buttons everywhere.
Come on, you bastards,
you're wasting my time and you know it!

I talk to socks.
Careful, you little bastards, if I slip here
I could crack my skull!

I talk to my boots.
Come on, you clodhoppers,
you used to fit me perfectly.

I talk to zips.
Pull yourselves together, wretches,
you're not even trying.

I talk to my sleeves.
You bastards, this is like
wrestling an invisible man.

And no matter
how I try
to tie my tie,
I can not
knot the
knot.

Listening to Wagner

For Shelagh Kareda

You said My late husband was listening to Wagner
when he said Now I will look at your poetry
(and I thought *Ah before* he was late!)
and you said I wrote it five years ago
and you wouldn't read it
and he said It is not always the time for poetry
but now *is* the time

and *I* said Excuse me
but that is a great opening line
and you said What is?
and I said My late husband was listening to Wagner
and you said Ah yes May I use it?
and I said Of course you may…
when it is the time!

Long Distance

It's for you – you said – sounds really far off.
Half asleep, I thought maybe a dead person
on the phone – one of our parents, perhaps,
with some urgent otherworldly message.

Through fizzing silence, a confused voice emerged.
Mine. *Hello*, I tried, but no answer came.
Then from blinding darkness burst
a hallucination of nightmare clarity.

Glaring with eyes of radiant black,
it made as if to snatch my phone. I loosed
a stunning double-kick, felt the smooth damp
weight – and screamed, *Devil!*

A warm hand on my arm
stirred me sweetly. I slumped back
onto the pillow, smile muscles
agitating the darkness…

With the foul sense of evil
still strong, the lifeline
of your touch wrested me
from a violent dream!

Often have I tried to think
a world that might come next.
None, I normally conclude – but this
close call has given me pause.

Look at the Speed!

We rattled along in our clumsy craft, fifteen sub-
teenagers bussed daily to a distant school.
Out of contact with the larger universe, we
talked, argued, and read. Epidemic enthusiasms
swept our community – stamps, foreign coins,
battles waged on travelling chess sets.
The Schoolboy's Pocket Book,
fuelled us with facts on capital cities,
constellations, sport and speed records.

Hobson was a trainspotter.

For twenty miles our route followed one side
or the other of the Carlisle-Edinburgh line,
driving Hobson to clamber the seats recklessly
for a prime view. Whenever a train
steamed alongside, he could not resist crying out,
Look at the speed!

Immune at first, I soon found myself staring
at each train that pushed past into the future
with such awesome intent. Eventually
the whole crew of us were on the lookout,
ready for the liberating roar:
Look at the speeed, Hobson!

In the summer holiday I cycled down
to Carlisle station. A penny platform ticket
allowed me to wander at will amid
the ominous clanking and hissing
of the behemoths.

(contd.)

Passengers, grey behind smutted windows,
sat toward the north or toward the south,
all wanting to be somewhere else.
They gazed into newspapers,
or peered outside –
perhaps even wondering what
that schoolboy was up to.

I was gaping,
gaping at immeasurable power:
the writhing muscles of smoke,
the jets of steam, the great
driving wheels taller than me
that slipped in agonies –
-gonies of impatience –
-patience as the locomotives –
-motives strained
to get under way…

And oh blast it, there was Hobson
with his blasted notebook, beaming.

Networking

    See
    what
    happens as
    your network
    to and fro grows:
    it's not just who you know,
    it's who who you know knows.

Mahmoud, Master of the World

The postgrad degree taxed him
less than a long walk.
Girls flocked to this soft-spoken
scholar, tall and understanding,
whose dark eyes smiled easily.
Even men recognized his splendour.

With five full days
of crucial exams now over
he pushed his fists into the air.
I am master of the world!

But people were watching,
Mahmoud told us another day.
Three times the same man
had looked at him on the bus; someone
threw stones at the window of his flat;
beggars were agents of the Shah.

Our cheery ministrations, our
fresh mastery of tensor calculus,
failed to loosen his knot of fears.

He started on a PhD, while we
developed our uncomplicated
lives. Multiplying threats shook
his confidence, tightened his smile.
That one's heading for trouble,
somebody said, *like a car
disappearing in the rearview mirror.*
We were too well to understand
his affliction, and within months
Mahmoud was lost to us.

A tempting rumour grew
from whisper toward truth –
excusing our neglect and
calming our concerns:
his family must have
talked him back to Tehran!

But we didn't know –
we didn't even know
what to hope. No news
ever reached us.
It very much seemed the world
had turned upon its gentle master.

Memorias Mexicanas

After two weeks on the Mexican coast with friends,
it took two weeks back at home to adjust
to their absence – to forget the daily four-hour
margarita-powered happy hours;

and two weeks to accept that a shining sun
can be bitter cold; mittens and boots are precious;
and unwelcome tasks unattended at home
remain unwelcome – and at home.

But pah - a trifling price paid!
The joys of companionship and discovery
that so filled fourteen days of our past
have added as many to our future.

The sand is sometimes wet and firm, sometimes
dry and soft: the undertow soothing or aggressive.
A careless colossus, I stride through a school of fish
flickering in the shallows.

A group of black cloaked vultures
on a deserted patch of beach shuffle
and nod, and plot some imminent villainy.

Emerging out of stillness, an iguana – strange enough
to cause a swift backward step – splays its unhurried way
across the dense canopy of shrubs, with a heavy, wet
rubberiness that is almost palpable.

A squadron of vintage pelicans lumbers by above the waves,
till they collapse and drop like broken kites, folding wings
at the last instant to become – in one surgical splash –
lethal; then lurch back to the sky with bulging beaks.

Tidal inrushes lick at the legs of a glistening
sun-polished sylph, who walks along the beach,
her tiny radio whispering into the soft air.

Boat-tailed grackles, private as London businessmen –
umbrellas at the ready, eyes black dots in yellow circles –
hop from foot to foot in search of quick gain.

The hoary souvenir vendor wraps a shawl tentatively
over a majestic blonde. She taps her languid foot – till
Uno, dos, tres, y cuatro thumps from the nearby dance class,
Uno, dos, tres, y cuatro.

Past the sightseers' impertinent catamaran, grey whales flow.
A calm patch remains on the surface when they dive,
like the silence that follows a striking thought.

The sea has been blue – green – grey and now
the evening sun unrolls a shimmering silver carpet
that comes almost to our feet.

Of Words and Truth

For Patrick Schindler,
mathematician and lawyer, 1941-2014.

In *Tense Logic for Discrete Future Time,*
March 1970, Patrick wrote:
an identical relation in a universal algebra
can be formulated in an abstract manner
by the use of the notion of a *word.*
Word can be recursively defined:

    (i)   a free element is a word;

    (ii)   a symbol for a nullary operation is a word;

    (iii)   if $\omega \in \Omega$, ω is *n*-ary, and $w_1, w_2, \ldots, w_n$ are words,
           then $w_1 w_2 \ldots w_n \omega$ is a word.

Forty-four years on,
his hair flourishes cheerfully,
even as his body is closing down.
Patrick is still concerned with
words – words and, indeed, truth –
enlivened often with humour
that can whisk you from courtroom to
brigands' lair in the wink of an eye.

His stories are unstoppable as ever:
neither can they be sped up by urging
nor slowed by a question. If interrupted,
he simply restates the last few words
and presses forward once again.

Approaching his end, he might lapse
into a short silence, eyes might slowly close.
His mind is re-buffering, and at any moment
he will resume the conversation. Today
he *defied criticism of diminished acuity* by
slipping *vicissitude* into a sentence, then *obeisance*.

An imminent legal triumph led him to observe
at least he would be going out on a high note.
That's funny, I said, I was just reading
about the composer Louis Vierne, who went out
on a low note – he had a stroke during an organ recital,
that left one foot sounding a prolonged and melancholy E.

Blending the elegance of algebra
with the algebra of elegance,
it is possible to draw from complexity
beauty – beauty and, indeed, truth –
in which delicate alchemy Patrick
for so long found particular joy.

Once...

Once before there was anything anywhere,
there occurred a bang that no one heard.

Once each oak tree was an acorn that fitted a squirrel's paw.

Once every butterfly crept like a caterpillar,
oblivious to its own exquisite future.

Once every poem was an unlimited silence, an immeasurable
void awaiting the consequences of a poet's work.

Once pictures hung on silent walls: centuries later they took
on movement, and theatre screens gave us music, love, laughter,
and tears...

Once each grandparent was a soft, smiling, defenseless baby,
with no inkling of the joys and jitters to come.

Once each omelet was a couple of potential chickens,
each hamburger

part of a living cow.

Before sliced bread was invented,
no one knew what the greatest thing was better than.

Before music, people had no idea
what they were not hearing.

Today will be yesterday tomorrow:
let it not be too soon forgotten.

Secs Toots

I think myself a thinking person –
there's always so much
heaving and frothing in my head.

This morning I was trying to
remember something I didn't want to forget
before it was too late, and a bubble

of lucidity broke the surface of cogitation.
I thumbed a quick note into my smart phone.
The task felt already half-completed.

Later I checked my Action List,
and was surprised to read the words:
Secs Toots.

I could not guess the original behind this
enigmatic auto-correction. For one who
imagines himself imaginative this was a blow.

My wife and I were preparing for a
garden party under the wisteria.
"What do you think of 'Secs Toots'?" I asked.

"Not the time, not the place,"
she said at once,
"and don't forget the napkins."

Maybe it would sell on a T-shirt,
I was thinking, maybe a trendy button.

"Forget what, my dear?"

One Idea

When he hit the wall at fifteen miles,
the world shrivelled,
his consciousness sloughed off
the newly irrelevant –

other runners, the weather, time,
the Marathon itself –
till he alone was left,
peering out of his sorry soul

with understanding focused by pain,
stripped of all past and pretension,
holding just one idea –
to run to the end.

For a two-hour eternity
he clung to that idea,
and completed the race
a transformed man.

Years later, when I look
into her eyes, the world shrinks,
my consciousness sloughs off
the newly irrelevant –

other people, the weather,
time, her very words,
till only she and I are left –
peering into each other's souls

with vision sharpened,
stripped of all past and pretension,
holding just one idea:
to love each other to the end.

However long this new eternity,
I remember clearly still
that distant marathon, and remain
a man transformed.

Quiet Taste

He is dipping into his new book.

The bus stops, the doors inhale –
four boisterous young men burst in,
squabbling – about boots.
They sprawl and rant, they own the bus.

Camouflage jacket a bit of a mockery, he thinks,
tentatively reopening the book. He senses a node
of watchful stillness: the tall cadet – the one who
spit-polishes his boots – asks what he's reading.

It's a new poetry collection.

Whereupon the cadet drops
into the seat beside him. The bus
rumbles and shakes
along Eglinton Avenue.

Final year at military school, he says,
and firmly resolved against army careers:
he'll not march to their drum despite
his father's billowing rage.

The others are arguing now
with the cheerful bombast of
facile conviction – which SUV
kicks the biggest ass.

Eyeing the book again, the cadet professes
a quiet taste for poetry. Writes a bit himself.
Nobody's really that different from us: (his eyes close)
it's misunderstanding makes everything worse.

The bus has reached Mount Pleasant.
Three of them clatter like thirty
down the steps. The would-be poet shakes hands,
and leaps at the last moment for the door.

Reconciliation

Mrs Shyke next door screamed.
I had caused a low fence along the lot line,
precisely located to discourage
her flowerbed's persistent invasion.
She could not hear through her fury
and stamped off to call a lawyer.
Vot I can do? her husband shrugged,
She is my vife!

We came home late one night and parked
in the driveway. I carried the baby upstairs.
A pungency pursued me into her room…
Something soft was clinging
to my shoe.

Daylight revealed my footprint in the evidence
beside the car, with more on the rear door.
Not the doings of our dogs – in a chain-link run
they could escape only under fear of lightning –
but of our other neighbour's unfettered mongrel.

That afternoon, I saw Mrs Shyke at work
on her front lawn with weed killer and hose.
I stormed over with a new father's determination.
Mrs Shyke,
you have thrown dog shit at my car.
Some was tramped into the baby's room.
You know it was not from my dogs –
and I think you're a filthy! nasty! old! bitch!

She gaped, holding her breath a long time.

Get out of my garden!
You're trespassing.
I'll have my lawyer...
And she turned the toxic hose on me.

For the next ten years we were
inaudible, invisible,
Mrs Shyke and I,
we did not exist.

Then one ruthless January morning
I saw her – by now a widow –
in a shabby fur coat
struggling with the drifts,
and finally I did the decent thing.

In the summer she resurrected
an old canvas deckchair,
and called to me across the fence
to admire her paint job.

Mrs Shyke, heavy with age,
eased herself into the chair.
There was an abrupt bathroom sound
as the canvas ripped and dumped her
on the grass. The white framework
pinioned her in a wreck
of struts and stripes. She trembled
with laughter, while the pain
in my ribs squeezed up tears.
An uncommon joint effort
at last restored her to her feet.

Years later, Mrs Shyke pouring vodka shots,
we remembered the fence, the dogs,
the weed killer, the deckchair.

She's long dead now.

Sixteen Dimensions

To honour sixteen dimensions of love,
a surprise Valentine dinner,
served severally in a variety of vessels.

Tastes, textures, tints, temperatures…
for the complexity and
dependencies of marriage:
sixteen for the essential twoness
of connubial joy, being
two
times two
times two
times two.

An onion to start, sliced on lines of latitude,
spelling oooo all over the chopping board:
half a red pepper similarly cut, fried in olive oil.
Cilantro leaves gently prised from their stalks,
and fennel (those silent bagpipes
of the vegetable kingdom) diced,
boiled soft, added to the frying pan ~
the whole served in an ornate dish
alive with butterflies and flowers.

Four long lettuce leaves rolled intact, each tied
with a curling red ribbon ~ on a square glass plate:
mayonnaise in individual red eggcups.

A dozen Brussels sprouts, outer leaves removed,
stems cross-cut, boiled *al dente* ~ in a glass coffee mug.

Pale celery sticks chosen fresh and crisp ~
reaching out of a craquelure pottery vase from China.

A yam, peeled, chopped to a convenient size,
boiled: frozen corn added for two minutes ~
in a grey-brown candy bowl.

Sliced mushrooms fried in butter with sesame seeds ~
in an earthenware drinking vessel, hand-made.

Green beans, trimmed, and boiled ~
stacked upright in a small cream jug.

Piquant pickled vegetables ~
in a pink porcelain poetry-prize jar,
with imitation antique Scottish coffee spoon.

A pair of veggie burgers,
microwaved for three minutes ~
on sensible dinner plates.

Foil-wrapped low-calorie chocolate fudge ~
in a carved cherrywood box.

Wine more golden than white ~
in our wedding-present glasses.

Sleep

Sleep peels
the person
from the body.
Until the instant of waking, flesh and bones
are going through a dry run for death.
Sleep is practice for death,
is like death without the loss.

I slept first in the arms
of a twenty-four-year-old woman,
before being granted a small space
in my brother's room.

On the lumpy sagging mattresses
of school dormitories, on pillows
like sandbags, I laid my shivering misery.
Rather the dripping tents of cloudy holidays,
the open cabin by a stream where milk pails stood.

Once I fell asleep on a beach, while the cruel French sun
flayed my unseasoned shoulders. Another time, hitching
by night in Wales and out of rides, I worked my shape
into a roadside gravel heap – and there slept,
till galvanized by the early morning
screech of peacocks behind estate walls.

I have drifted off during sermons, during an oboe recital,
in the backseat of a car; have slept under the moon
in a Scottish field, and all night on an unforgiving
picnic bench in South Dakota.

The joy of sleep precedes actual sleep
by moments, like the au revoir
of the sun's slide below the horizon.
Inferred later by dawning
wakefulness, the thing itself
remains beyond experience.

Let me then night after night
share with my wife
a queen-size bed, and so
embrace again
the next new day.

Snow Shovel

The heavy overnight fall was a
surprise. He opened the front door
onto a morning without colour
or sound or shape, barely noticing
the cardinal on the telephone wire.

Moving the minimum amount of snow
he found a rhythm of economy,
felt even pleasure in his new shovel.
The job was almost done when
an ugly yellow municipal snowplow
came grinding round the corner

and raised an instant dense, dirty-white
wall waist-high across his driveway.

He flung his shovel at the cab window
big-banging a starburst of cracks
driving the cardinal in a red wound across the sky
and bringing the snowplow
to an abrupt stop.

The driver –
full orange
winter gear,
battle-scarred
safety helmet –
climbed out,
hitched up
his pants,
swaggered
over.

What the hell
're ya doin'!
Sorry, I didn't think…
I'm reporting this one,
yes sir.

Jesus! A minute ago
everything had been great.
Now all he could see was cracks
spreading lazily outwards,
obliterating by degrees
the startled face of the driver.

Unless it was,
like, a branch,
sticking out –
ya know?

There were no trees in sight.
He took off his mittens and fumbled
a couple of twenties from his pocket.

A branch, what lousy luck, he said,
reaching across the snow.
More careful next time, eh?

The driver swung up into the cab,
and raised his coffee mug.
Releasing a noisome grey cloud,
the plow lurched off.

(contd.)

A crunch sounded
through the engine noise –
his snow shovel,
under a back wheel.

Served me damn right,
he told us later.
And I've watched
that starburst slowly
wipe out the driver
a hundred times since then.

Some Day Soon

For Casper Fertuck.

On my way to see a new person,
and suddenly I'm friends with anybody
holding a baby or pushing a stroller.
The highway snackbar girl
says *How are you today?*
I'm a grandfather (can't she tell?) –
since 3:37 this morning!

In seven pounds eleven, the full heft
and wonder of human life.
Where was he one year ago,
where will he be, and be, and be?

Already he peeps from tiny eyes
with such authority.
See his hair of golden silk,
ears artfully shaped, mouth so active.
And those long fingers – here,
give him back to me!

We two are going to be so busy. Some day soon
I'll push your stroller to Nanny Goat Gardens
and tell you about turnips & parsnips & potatoes
and introduce you to friends, shopkeepers, perfect strangers
and carry you on my shoulders to watch the band
and come to your birthday party
and read you *The Little Prince*
and sit with you at concerts
and show you stupendous paintings at the gallery
and clap at your recital and cheer for your team.

(contd.)

We will laugh at ourselves and the world,
and you will grow into somebody
nobody can imagine.

Storytelling

"The older I get, the better I used to be." – Lee Trevino

(I) 1962 Summer, remembered 10 years later

Pitched and tossed across the Channel
into a solo hitchhiking venture,
my highschool languages, so full
of attitude in the classroom, cowered
below the threshold of speech.
I travelled by thumb, bought baguettes
and fruit by index finger.

Sitting in a corner of a Paris Youth Hostel
I read *A Concise History of Modern Art,*
while a spirited crowd materialized
out of a Gauloise fog across the room.
Beneath my carapace of self-composure
I ached to chat and drink and laugh.

For a month I pressed on from one destination
to another, seldom pausing to try the coffee,
taste the beer, investigate the charcuterie –
too English still, too low on savoir faire,
to savour the Frenchness of France.

(II) 1962 Summer, remembered 30 years later

Somehow I found myself in a night club
in the Quartier Pigalle – where Pepita
coyly disclosed her charms, to music
that still re-echoes in my memory.

(contd.)

For the first time ever, I was looking at
a naked woman unconstrained
by plinth or picture frame,
stunned by the overwhelming
reality of the female form.

I made my haphazard way to the south coast,
logging occasional adventures en route:
such as a humbling walk with a friend's dog,
to which I was instructed to speak
in French. *Viens ici, Floqui!*
A clearer sense was slowly forming
of how *other* other cultures could be.

From a desolate roadside a couple
rounding out their honeymoon rescued me
(what were they thinking?) and
drove me five hundred kilometres
back to Paris. We talked
till late in their apartment,
drowsy with Courvoisier and Berlioz.
They deserved to live happily.

(III) 1962 Summer, remembered 50 years later

University at the time, without money,
plans, or fear – but hungry for Europe.
Soon mastered the language thing,
sliding easily between bad French,
bad German, and the bad English
that makes it easier for foreigners.

Bon vivant, and on and on!
Those three-hour dinners, the wine, the cheese –
O God, don't talk about the cheese,
it's another whole art form.

And the people you met – came from
anywhere, talked about anything.
Down on the Mediterranean,
afraid further resistance might cause
lifelong regret, I succumbed to temptation…
Pampelonne, a beach outside Saint-Tropez
where clothing was kept to a bare minimum,
promised – oh yes, and delivered –
stunning revelations.

A prudent cooling-off period
before dashing into the water – then,
chilled and chastened, I strolled
the crowded beach looking keenly
in every direction for Nicole
(didn't know anyone called Nicole!).

This glorious finale to
two decades of innocence
taught more than a roomful of art books.
I grew up five years in a week,
and never looked back on France
but with delight.

Summer Sports

How convenient for smuggling books
into the dormitory, those capacious
cord jackets that zipped up the front.
School rules harsh as Edinburgh Castle
forbade reading in bed, or talking
between lights-out and the rising bell.

In summer, though, the bonus
Sunday morning one-hour lie-in
offered the chance of a few chapters.
That year, curious at last about love,
I was easily drawn to the
English village dramas of a
John Moore romance.

That cherished green carpet
only the finest elevens might tread –
the disgruntled mower,
trailing a wisp of oily smoke;
the smell of cut grass; groundsmen
laying down the definitive
white lines of a cricket field.

First Team matches we had to attend, as if
even proximity might make gentlemen of us.
Games developed dreamily – the acolytes,
elegant in the days before helmets, wore
white shirts, white flannels, white boots.
And the two white-coated umpires,
broadened by surplus sweaters around the waist,
judged like Old Testament gods.

No great fans, my friends and I, we sprawled
on tartan rugs, talking, snoozing,
reading – permitted by venerable tradition –
in the precious sun. Easy to tune out
the stubborn *dok* of bat on ball,
the odd *Howzat!* School's ponderous
formalities were no match for the
early loves of *Midsummer Meadow*.

Team Player

I always smile and say good morning at the office.

My desk looks busy and tidy, efficient but not anal.

The Organization Chart is pinned up beside my computer
with my boss highlighted, also the picture of the president
shaking my hand for helping with the Christmas party.

It takes five minutes to wash and refill my coffee cup.
Three times a day makes quarter of an hour,
they owe me that much!

When there's a collection for a wedding or a retirement
or a baby I give the amount I think they'd give if I
was getting married or retiring or having a baby.

If everyone is laughing about something I laugh too.
That's teamwork.

But buzzwords and acronyms are unfair to people
who don't know what they mean. Like MYOB.

When they say to leave early because of the snowstorm
I keep working till there's hardly anyone left –
it makes our department look good.

I bought an echinocactus grusonii (botanical name!)
for my desk. When rain is forecast in Phoenix, Arizona,
I sprinkle water on my cactus.

We've been told not to send useless emails.
I cc my boss so he will know my emails
are not useless and I'm doing good work.

All in all, on the whole – I enjoy going to the office.
Except when they tease me about my cheese sandwiches.
Or make a joke I can't understand.
Or don't recognize me in the corridor.
Or forget to invite me along for the pub lunch...

To: Department_List
From: Admin
Subject: Sniggering

Hope you enjoyed your lunch.
I'll be out of the office for a month.
Phone me for personal salary insights.
I've a great memory for figures.

The Golden Fly

*The indented lines are Asoke Chakravarty's
original poem, The Golden Fly.*

    I killed a golden fly
that bustled unasked into my dream –
    and was punished,
careless cruelty the charge.
    Not exactly an imprisonment,
but for the mind
    a life sentence,
confined to my own head
    without parole.
My busyness resembles the fly's,
    more like it
as each year falls behind.
    The prison is a jewel
that reflects but does not shine,
    disrupting my sedate life.
Impossible to unremember
    I killed a golden fly,
and one day too shall meet
    an enchanting golden death.

The Night Is Darker Now

The Facts:

*Minutes into the Toronto Symphony Orchestra -
Mendelssohn Choir* Messiah *at Roy Thomson Hall,
December 2011, a patron at front row centre began to talk
loudly. Her companion got up and left the hall. She followed
soon after.*

The Fiction:

Heavy-coated, motionless amid hurrying pedestrians,
a man is studying the billboard by the concert hall.

He steps into a nearby bar to warm up. Perched
at a window, he is pleased with his single malt.

A woman, thirties or forties, makes her way
across the room, flashing a cautious smile.
—Mind if I…? Waiting for a friend!

She sets down her empty glass, pulls up a stool.
—What can I get you?
—Same as yours would be great.

She swirls the ice cubes. Good looking woman,
slender wrists, make-up generous. More like fifty.

He glances outside. —It's getting colder.
She shivers agreeably. —Ooh, this is strong.
—Good scotch!

(contd.)

He says how he's missing his wife in Thunder Bay,
tells of the expected grandchild.
—We're hoping for Christmas Day.
—My Gabe's been gone fifteen years. She takes
a tissue from her purse. I've never got used to it.

He orders another round.
—They shouldn't be sending you from home so close
to Christmas. It isn't right, she shakes her head, it's not right.

He picks up the menu. Been a hard week.
—How about some calamari?
—Lovely!

She points out the crowds heading for the hall.
—Why don't we go too? he says. The Messiah.
—'Messiah, the night is darker now,' she warbles, remembering
something from way back.

He takes her arm to cross King Street. Their luck
is in, someone has extra tickets, right at the front.
Not cheap – but then he hasn't heard the Messiah since…
he hasn't ever heard the whole thing!

—Look at this place, she says. Everyone so old.
They find their seats easily.
—Lots of leg-room, he says.

—That stuff makes you sleepy. Is there popcorn?
Her eyelids are drooping. He studies his program.

The music wakens her. Some of the players are
really close, a man is singing in a slow high voice.
—Hey, what's going on? George, Jim…,
she stares about, this is crazy.

—Shhh.
—You said they'd play the Hallelujah Chorus!

He hushes her again.
—Leave me alone, she shrugs, not even trying to whisper.
I can't listen to this, and she fumbles in her purse for
something.

As the music continues, one of the players sets down
his cello, crouches at the front of the stage,
and taps her shoulder with his bow.
He gestures for silence, and returns to his seat.

Her companion gathers his coat and scarf.
—Hey, where…? But he is off, head down, to the nearest exit.
He thrusts $20 into the usher's hand. —Put her in a cab.

Minutes later she flounces through the same door.
—Oh, Madam, the gentleman left this for your taxi.
—*Gentleman!*

A few streets away, relief surges through him –
better than the scotch, better than the calamari.
No one will ever know, he thinks, Hallelujah! –
though now I may never hear the whole thing.

The Very Word

Sometimes a cloud drifts across
the matrix of my vocabulary
and blots out the very word
I'm looking for.

Vestibule is hard for me – and that person
who isn't an accountant – but my mental
thesaurus often kicks in in the nick
of time (*lobby,* it whispers, *actuary*).

But surely you can't blot out
a word that isn't there! So it's not
actually *gone,* it's just obscured by a
cerebral blip of some sort.

Naturally, words and names can be
elusive at any time: that's why we have
the *thingummy* and the *widget,* that's why
So-and-so and *Who's-it.*

My friend – um – she isn't
an inch over four foot eight…
Know what they used to call me at school? she said,
They used to call me Microbe!

Well, Microbe was telling me how
she spotted her massage therapist
in a restaurant one day. She gave
a big *Hello* that caused one of those

sudden group silences. The guy
stared back vacuously.
What, said Microbe,
*don't you recognize me
with my clothes on?*

Then she saw it wasn't him…

Just age, do you suppose,
or is she getting that thing?

The Thing About Apostrophe's

Fretting about apostrophes'
like scratching an itch
distracts you briefly from
global warming, the price of gas,
neighbourhood parties you're not at…

To notice others' errors' is to
underline how exceptional *you* are,
while sweetly stimulating
your irritation zone.
How good is that!

Apostrophes? Keep 'em 'comin!

Viewpoints

At the window table he was happily
observing the December crowd outside,
                            when she spoke.
I feel like a goldfish in a bowl.

His gaze panned to the billows
of approaching cloud, his smile sagged.
The persona concocted to match his
intricate self-concept began to blur.

She was a certain beauty, confident
for all her bashful ways, unlikely to be improved
by the radiance of his fantasies. He
would always be looking *into* the fishbowl.

They locked eyes across the deep mis-fit –

then turned aside, and with hardly a word
sipped at the last of their wine.

Tricks My Father Taught Me

A bow   tie not
yet tied hangs   limp and feckless:
but suitably fastened,   it becomes a striking
emblem, organic rather than geometric, more
forceful by far than a puny factory readymade.
Even Prince Charming   chose to tie his own,
knowing exuberance   cannot simply be
strapped   on.

A
l
s
o
there is an
ingenious way to cut an
apple whose mastery needs
practice. Two congruent three
pointed partners fit snug on sev
eral surfaces. When pressed tog
ether the deeply satisfying join
can not be seen. A perfect
match of complex shapes,
a whole in one.

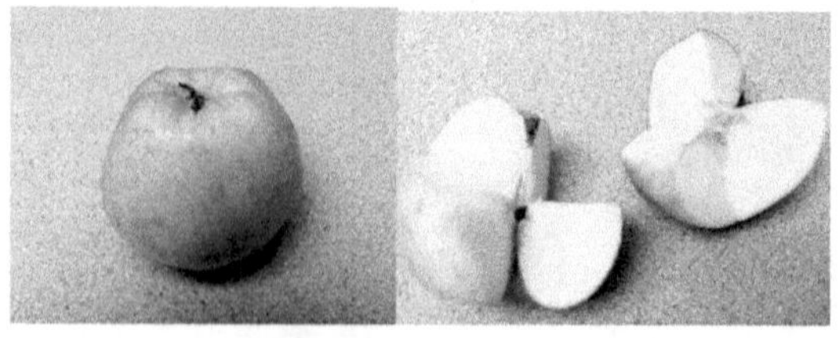

Warming

For Brent Wardrop.

Early commuters mute at
the bus stop, still as inukshuks.
Cold – this is the coldest cold –
pierces winter clothes with icy needles.

An SUV jerks to a halt by the sign.
Radio cuts, sweatered driver
with handful of papers bounds
three steps to house behind.

Who's he think…? But in seconds,
Hey, he's back, *it's cold out here,*
rubbing his hands, *anyone want
a ride down town?*

I'll come, pipes up
one weather-beaten turncoat –
and into the Range Rover
I climb.

Where are you headed?
Any subway station will do –
but the driver insists,
and makes a fearless U-turn.

As we swing and surge through irritable traffic,
he tells of his passion for marketing.
And you? he asks. Retired engineer,
doing communications work.

(contd.)

How do you spend your spare time?
Just published a book of poetry.
Poetry! What do you write about? Now
he turns to me. *Where do you find your ideas?*

Suddenly I could talk for an hour –
but here we are, my place of work. I find him
a copy of the book in my briefcase.
We shake hands. *Looking forward to this!*

It's not *that* cold outside.

Weight

My heart, exhausted
by the tribulations
of early love, responds
with sorry throbs to
your daylong absence.

The remorseless tide of evening
weighs upon me as light drains.
Beached in my solitary room
I will my last energy into
a hushed *Good night.*

Grateful slumber,
that brings us
sooner close!
Time murmurs
for a second,
for a century –

till my phone shatters
the nullity of sleep.
I grope, I grab. Look,
twelve oh five displayed
by that imperturbable agent:
barely ten minutes stretched
between whisper and *At last!*

Happiness makes the ponderous
buoyant, makes darkness light:
there is no up without down,
no levity without gravity.
Throb has become sparkle.

Winning the Toss

When I was twelve I didn't really get the point
of horses. Bicycles were much more predictable,
and you could see how they worked.

For a few lucky months, my sister and mother,
who shared a passion for the animal, had the care of
a neighbour's pony – feeding and grooming,
mucking out the stable, and riding Pommelle,
every day. Sometimes timetables clashed,
and I was called in to exercise the pony.

Two zealous coaches refreshed me on
matters of saddling up, adjusting the stirrups,
and other essential equestrian practices.
(Much easier to get a bike out of a shed.)

With a head too small
for my mother's riding helmet
and too large for my sister's,
I was willing to go unprotected.

There were times I admit when I sensed
the thrill of being in charge of a powerful animal.
To hear her snort or whinny,
to give her a friendly pat on the neck
(did she know it was friendly?) or look into her
limpid eyes, was to feel the heat and strength
of the creature, and glimpse a rival determination
(did she know I was the boss?).

One afternoon I rode out of the village, past the ditch
that used to supply the wriggling miracle
of frogspawn for our jam jars –
and along a cinder track into farm country.
A gentle hill led down to fields and pastures
in the fertile flatland of the Caldew river.

The track passed over a railway line that served
small Cumbrian towns and villages. The simple
arched bridge was just wide enough for a tractor.
Its sides, made of sandstone blocks,
were a couple of feet high. From here I always
admired how the railway's calculated contours
contrasted with the winding course of the river.

As we were crossing the bridge that day, I saw
one of the new diesel trains approaching.
I halted Pommelle so I could watch.
The train closed in at a surprising speed,
engulfing us in a blinding blast
of acrid fumes as it roared beneath.

At this explosion of horrors, Pommelle
reacted without hesitation. She threw me off
and galloped away. There was a thump
like a kick on the head and the sky darkened.

I got to my feet, and brushed cinders
from stinging knees and elbows.
Halfway up the hill Pommelle waited calmly,
allowing me to take charge again. What if she had
tossed me the other side? I hardly dared think.

(contd.)

It was a struggle to remount – but my breathing
gradually steadied, and I forced myself to sit
straight-backed as we made our way home.

Whenever I looked into Pommelle's eyes
after that day, the depths of silent wisdom
remained mysterious and formidable.
Not at all like a bike.